Floral Illustrations of the Seasons

Consisting of the Most Beautiful, Hardy and Rare Herbaceous Plants, Cultivated in the Flower Garden

M. Roscoe

Plate 1. *Crocus*.

Drawn from Nature by M.R. Junr.

Engraved by R. Havell

CROCUS mæsiacus.

Common Yellow Crocus.

Class and Order.—Triandria Monogynia.

Syn. *Curt.Bot.Mag.*, p. 1111.

Crocus langeæflorus. *Salisbury Par.Lon.* vol. ii., tab. 106.

Bulb small—leaves numerous, radical, linear, lanceolate—flower enclosed with the leaves in a membranous sheath—corolla yellow, divided into six oval-shaped petals, the three outer divisions beautifully marked with green—stamens three—filaments short—anthers sagittate—style one—stigma divided into three parts.

The species here figured is the earliest and best known in our gardens. It was introduced into this country in the year 1629, and derives its specific denomination from the ancient name of that part of Europe where it abounds in a wild state. Numerous varieties of the genus are constantly raised from seed, but the number of distinct species do not exceed ten or twelve. The cultivation of these plants is attended with no difficulty whatever: they will grow in any soil or situation; and the C. mæsiacus increases so rapidly as to require frequent parting. The different varieties make a beautiful display in the months of February and March, if placed in alternate patches in the flower border, and produce a brilliant effect when expanded by the warmth of the sun. The most desirable for a flower garden are the following species and their varieties:—

Crocus vernus.	Crocus susianus.
—— versicolor.	—— sulphureus.
—— nudiflorus.	—— sativus.

—— biflorus.   —— autumnalis.

Pl. 1.

Plate 2. Hepatica Triloba.
Drawn from Nature by M.R.

Junr. *Engraved by R. Havell*

HEPATICA triloba.

Common Blue Hepatica.

Class and Order.—Polyandria Polygynia.

Syn. Hepatica triloba. *Pursh, N. A. F., vol.* ii., *p.* 391.

Root fibrous—leaves radical, three-lobed, on long petioles—stem simple, erect, pubescent—one-flowered calyx of three leaves—corolla blue—six petals, oval-shaped—stamens numerous, fixed to the receptacle—styles many—stigmas obtuse.

The blue variety of the Hepatica triloba, which blooms about March, is one of our most beautiful Spring flowers, and is more readily cultivated than any of the other kinds. According to Pursh, "It is a native of Canada, and is found in woods, and on the sides of fertile and rocky hills." The double variety of this plant is less common in our gardens, and the single white variety is rare. These plants like a loamy soil, and eastern exposure—and should be removed when they are in blossom. The roots do not bear to be often separated; and if divided into small pieces are frequently lost: but if left undisturbed in a congenial situation, they will attain great luxuriance. Miller says the single varieties are easily propagated by seed; but our more modern gardeners do not coincide in this opinion. The new leaves do not appear until after the flowers, though occasionally those of the preceding year retain their freshness, as in the figure here given. All the Hepaticas are ornamental.

Double blue.	Double pink.
Single pink.	Single white.

Plate 3. *Scilla Bifolia.*

Drawn from Nature by M.R.   *Engraved by R. Havell Jun[r.]*

SCILLA bifolia.

Two-leaved Squill.

Class and Order.—Hexandria Monogynia.

Syn. Scilla bifolia. *Eng. Fl., vol.* ii., *p.* 146.

Bulb oblong, oval—leaves two, radical, opposite, linear, lanceolate, about five or six inches long—peduncles short—corolla bright blue—petals six, oblong, spreading in the form of a star—stamens six, shorter than the petals—germen superior—styles short.

This beautiful plant is a native of the West of England, though rarely found. It likes a light soil, and should be grown in large patches, when it forms one of the greatest ornaments to our gardens in the month of March. The white variety also flowers about the same time, and forms a striking and beautiful contrast if placed alternately in the flower border. It is increased by offsets, which may be removed when the leaves decay. If this plant be covered with a hand-glass, when coming into bloom, it will expand more fully, and preserve the brilliancy of its colour. The Scilla maritima possesses peculiar medicinal properties. The most beautiful species are

Scilla amæna.	Scilla Italica.
—— Siberica.	—— Peruviana.
—— Verna.	—— præcox.

Pl. 3.

Plate 4. Narcissus Moschatus.

Drawn from Nature by M.R.   *Engraved by R. Havell Junr.*

NARCISSUS Moschatus.

Spanish Daffodil.

Class and Order.—Hexandria Monogynia.

Syn. Narcissus Moschatus. *Curt. Bot. Mag., p.* 1300.

Root bulbous—leaves radical, linear—twisted, glaucous—stem simple, erect—flowers solitary, issuing from a sheath, lanceolate—corolla cream colour, consisting of a tubular nectary, with a laciniated mouth, surrounded by six long tortuose petals—stamens six—pistil one, enclosed in the tube.

This plant is one of the least common and most beautiful of the genus, and is remarkable for the peculiar delicacy of its colour. It is a native of Spain, and was introduced into this country about the year 1759. It requires a light rich soil; and, like all other bulbs, ought only to be removed when the leaves decay. The plant grows from twelve to sixteen inches high, and flowers in April. The genus Narcissus is a very numerous and beautiful one, and affords a delightful variety. Some of the most ornamental are

N. bulbocodium.	N. triandrus.
— poeticus.	— tenuifolius.
— angustifolius.	— incomparibilis.
— biflorus.	— bicolor.
— odorus.	— minor.
— tenuior.	

Pl. 4.

Plate 5. *Erythronium Dens Canis.*

Drawn from Nature by M.R. Junr.

Engraved by R. Havell

ERYTHRONIUM dens canis.

Common Dog's-tooth Violet.

Class and Order.—HEXANDRIA MONOGYNIA.

Syn. Erythronium dens canis. *Curt. Bot. Mag.*, p. 5.

Root bulbous, oblong—leaves radical, broad, lanceolate, somewhat undulate, marked with brown—stem naked, erect—flowers solitary, drooping—corolla campanulate, composed of six equal oval-shaped petals, of a lilac hue, inclining to pink—stamens six, terminated by oblong purple anthers—germen superior—style longer than the stamens—stigma divided into three parts. When the flowers are fully expanded the petals are reflexed. The white variety differs only in the colour of the flower.

There are few plants more desirable for a flower garden than the Erythronium dens canis, and its white variety; and none contribute more to the beauty of our borders in the month of March, or beginning of April. It is a native of Hungary, and some parts of Italy, and was introduced into this country in the year 1596. These plants like a light soil, mixed with bog, and are propagated by offsets, which may be removed any time after the leaves decay; but the roots should not be kept long out of the ground, as they are liable to shrink. Miller mentions two species of the lilac Erythronium; but his distinctions, founded only on the breadth of the leaves, and colour of the flower, would not be sufficient to form a different species. It is, however, worthy of remark, that the leaves of those bulbs which do not bear flowers, are broader and rounder than the others. There are two other species, mentioned by Pursh, in his "Flora of North America," vol. i. p. 230, both bearing yellow flowers, one of which is occasionally seen in our gardens.—Erythronium Americanum.

Plate 6. *Adonis Vernalis.*

Drawn from Nature by M.R.

Engraved by R. Havell Jun.

ADONIS vernalis.

Perennial Adonis.

Class and Order.—Polyandria Polygynia.

Syn. Adonis vernalis. *Curt. Bot. Mag., p.* 134.

Root fibrous—stem branching, growing to the height of ten or twelve inches—leaves pinnate, pinnatified—calyx five segments, deciduous—flowers terminal—corolla yellow, composed of twelve or fourteen oval-shaped petals—stamens numerous—styles many—germen superior.

Though this plant has been long known in our gardens, having been introduced in the year 1629, it is by no means common. It is found wild on the mountains of Switzerland, and in different parts of Austria. It likes a rich loamy soil, and is increased by parting the roots; but to have it in perfection it should be grown in large patches, and seldom divided, when it makes a beautiful appearance in the flower garden in the months of March or April. In its native country, this plant does not exceed four inches in height, and the flowers are of a much more brilliant colour. There are two other species of Adonis, but they are seldom met with.

A. autumnalis.

— flammea.

Plate 7. *Primula Auricula.*

Drawn from Nature by M.R.   **Engraved by R. Havell Junr.**

PRIMULA auricula.

Auricula.

Class and Order.—Pentandria Monogynia.

Syn. Primula auricula. *Jacquin Flo. Aus.* 5, *t.* 415?

Root fibrous—leaves radical, ovate, dentate—base entire—stem simple, radical—flower terminal, corymbose—calyx five segments—corolla monopetalous, cream colour, slightly tinged with yellow, five segments, emarginate—stamens five—pistil one.

This plant is a native of Switzerland, and was introduced into this country about the year 1596. It is the parent of all the beautiful varieties of Auricula, which are now cultivated in our gardens. It grows low, and, like many of the genus, is suitable and ornamental for rock work. The Primulas flourish most in a mixture of loam, decayed leaves, and bog earth, and, like all Alpine plants, require a pure atmosphere. The leaves of this species are apt to vary in form, the margins occasionally being entire. Some of the most beautiful are the following:—

Primula nivalis.	Primula villosa.
—— cortusoides.	—— farinosa.
—— helvetica.	—— Scotica.
—— decora.	—— Pallasii.
—— integrifolia.	—— minima.
—— marginata.	

Plate 8. *Sanguinaria Grandiflora.*
Drawn from Nature by M.R.   *Engraved by R. Havell Jun[r.]*

SANGUINARIA grandiflora.

Large-flowered Bloodwort.

Class and Order.—POLYANDRIA MONOGYNIA.

Syn. *Lyon's MSS.*

Root tuberous, knobbed—leaves radical, lobed—lobes laciniated, light green, under surface reddish purple—veins red—enclosing the infant blossom, which gradually emerges from its folds—flower stem simple, erect, about six or eight inches in height—calyx two segments, convex, deciduous—corolla white—petals eight, oblong, obtuse—stamens many—style very short—germen superior, terminated by a stigma divided into two parts.

This beautiful species, which is much larger than the Sanguinaria Canadensis, was introduced into this country about the year 1812, by the late Mr. John Lyon, with several other valuable plants, collected by him in different parts of North America. It takes its name from the root, which, when broken, emits a red juice resembling blood, with which the Indians are said to paint themselves. Its blossoms are transient, and, like many other Spring flowers, require the warmth of the sun to expand them. It grows best in bog soil and a sheltered situation, and may be increased by parting its roots, which should be done in the Autumn, to prevent any check to its flowering in the following March or April. There is only another species, the S. Canadensis, above alluded to.

Pl. 8.

SUMMER.

Hail, gentle Summer! every mead
With thy fair robe of beauty spread
    To thee that beauty owes;
The smiling flowers with joy declare,
And loudly tell to Reason's ear,
    Whence all that beauty flows.
              Fawkes.

Plate 17. *Pæonia Tenuifolia.*

Drawn from Nature by M.R. Junr.

Engraved by R. Havell

PÆONIA tenuifolia.

Fine-leaved Pæony.

Class and Order.—POLYANDRIA TRIGYNIA.

Syn. Pæonia tenuifolia. *Curt. Bot. Mag., pl.* 926.

Root tuberous—stem erect, branching, growing to the height of one foot, or more—leaves numerous, biternate, linear—calyx five segments—flowers terminal—corolla deep scarlet—eight petals, orbicular, undulate—stamens many—anthers bright yellow—styles three—germen superior.

Though this beautiful plant has been so long known in our gardens, being introduced in the year 1756, it seldom grows luxuriantly, which perhaps may be accounted for by the liability of the roots to decay in cold wet soils. It is a native of Siberia, flowers in May, and makes a brilliant appearance when grown in large patches. The Pæonias grow best in a rich loamy soil, and may be increased by parting the roots, or by seed; by the latter means several most beautiful varieties have been raised of the Pæonia moutan, of which a full account may be seen in the "Hor. Soc. Trans.," vol. 6. This is a remarkably handsome genus. Some of the most ornamental are

P. odorata.
— sibirica.
— albiflora.
— Sabinii.
— peregrina.

P. rosea.
— moutan.
— papavaracea.
— corallina.
— humilis.

Plate 18. *Phlox Divaricata.*

Drawn from Nature by M.R. Junr.

Engraved by R. Havell

PHLOX divaricata.

Early-flowering Lychnidea.

Class and Order.—Pentandria Monogynia.

Syn. Phlox divaricata. *Curt. Bot. Mag., pl. 163. Pursh's Flo. N. A., vol. i., p. 150.*

Root fibrous—stem branching—leaves opposite, sessile, oblong oval, acute, undulate—flowers corymbose—peduncles short—calyx five segments, linear, acute—corolla monopetalous—five segments, emarginate, narrower at the base—pale blue—stamens five—style one—stigma divided into three parts.

The genus Phlox is perhaps one of the most beautiful cultivated in our gardens, and affords a delightful variety, its different species flowering all through the Summer and Autumn. The plant here figured is the earliest; and though it cannot boast of brilliancy, it is remarkable for the beautiful delicacy of its colour, and modest appearance. It grows low, seldom exceeding eight or ten inches in height, and is, on this account, very suitable for rock work. It flowers in May, likes a strong loamy soil, and is increased by parting the roots, or by cuttings. This species is a native of the mountains of Virginia, North America, and was brought into this country by the late Mr. Fraser. There are various others equally desirable for a flower garden. Amongst the most beautiful are

P. pyramidalis.	P. subulata.
— ovata.	— reflexa.
— carnea.	— amæma.
— nivalis.	— stolonifera.

— setacea.

Pl. 18.

Plate 19. *Anemone Palmata.*

Drawn from Nature by M.R. Junr

Engraved by R. Havell

ANEMONE palmata.

Cyclamen-leaved Anemone.

Class and Order.—POLYANDRIA POLYGYNIA.

Syn. Anemone palmata. *Bot. Reg. pl.* 200. *Persoon. Syn. Plan., vol. ii., p. 97.*

Root tuberous—leaves radical, cordate, suborbiculate, dentate—stem radical, clothed with a ferruginous hair—flower issuing from an involucrum, sessile, trifid—corolla yellow—petals about twelve, oblong, obtuse—stamens numerous—styles many—germen superior.

This is a most striking and ornamental species, and though it is said to have been introduced so far back as the year 1597, is still rare in our gardens. It is difficult to cultivate, perhaps requiring a little stronger soil than Anemonies generally do. When its roots have attained a great size, it should be removed or divided, as it is then liable to decay; few, however, are fortunate enough to cultivate it to such a state of luxuriance. It is perfectly hardy, though mostly treated as a frame plant. The under side of the lower radical leaves is tinged with a bright violet colour. The genus Anemone is a numerous one, and can boast of many ornamental species.

A. appennina.	A. sylvestris.
— hortensis.	— baldensis.
— patens.	— thalictroides.
— narcissiflora.	— pavonina.
— pratensis.	— pulsatilla.

Plate 20. *Pulmonaria Paniculata.*

Drawn from Nature by M.R.   *Engraved by R. Havell Junr.*

PULMONARIA paniculata.

Panicled Lungwort.

Class and Order.—PENTANDRIA MONOGYNIA.

Syn. Pulmonaria paniculata. *Curt. Bot. Mag., pl.* 2680.

Root tuberous—stem branched, one to two feet high—leaves ovate, oblong, acuminate, strongly nerved—panicles leafy—flowers drooping—calyx five segments—corolla funnel-shaped, contracted near the base—when arrived at maturity, of a brilliant blue—stamens five—style equal with the stamens—stigma obtuse—plant hispid.

This beautiful plant, according to the "Bot. Mag.," 2680, is a native of Hudson's Bay, and was "Originally introduced to the Kew Gardens by the late Dr. Solander, in 1778." It is still rare, and difficult to cultivate, though in congenial situations it will sow its seed, and increase abundantly; but the general method of propagating it is by parting the roots. The plant from which the annexed drawing was made grows luxuriantly in a cold, stiff soil, and has endured our severest winters without protection. It flowers in June; and though each blossom falls off almost as soon as it becomes perfect, there is a succession for a considerable time. The most beautiful species of this genus are—

      P. virginica.
      — davurica.

Plate 21. Campanula Pulla.

Drawn from Nature by M.R.

Jun.

Engraved by R. Havell

CAMPANULA pulla.

Russet Bell Flower.

Class and Order.—Pentandria Monogynia.

Syn. Campanula pulla. *Loddige's Bot. Cab., p. 554.*

Root fibrous—plant from two to three inches high—stem slender, radical, leafy, one-flowered—leaves very small, ovate, crenate, sessile, opposite—flowers terminal, drooping—calyx five segments—corolla purple, monopetalous, campanulate—margin five cleft—stamens five—style longer than the stamens—stigma divided into three parts—germen inferior.

This lovely little plant is a native of the mountains of Austria and Styria, and is particularly ornamental for rock work, to which it is well adapted by its low growth and general habit. It was introduced into this country about the year 1779, but is still very seldom met with. It is hardy, though like many Alpine plants is liable to be lost in the Winter unless protected, and it is therefore the safest plan either to keep it in a frame, or to cover it with dry leaves and a hand glass during Winter. It flowers in June, likes a light rich soil, and is increased by parting the roots. The genus Campanula is a very numerous one, consisting of upwards of sixty species: some of the most ornamental are—

C. peregrina.   C. barbata.
— carpatica.   — punctata.
— patula.   — Scheuchzeri.
— persicifolia.   — pyramidalis.
— capitata.   — azurea.

Plate 22. Œnothera Triloba.

Drawn from Nature by M.R.

Engraved by R. Havell Junr.

ŒNOTHERA triloba.

Dandelion-leaved Evening Primrose.

Class and Order.—OCTANDRIA MONOGYNIA.

Syn. Œnothera triloba. *Curt. Bot. Mag., pl.* 2566.

Root biennial? spindle-shaped—leaves radical, lyrate, dentate, smooth, middle rib strong—flower radical, rising from amongst the bright green leaves—calyx tubular—four segments, lanceolate, acute—corolla pale delicate yellow—petals four, slightly trilobed, undulate—stamens eight—filaments shorter than the petals—anthers oblong, bright yellow—style a little longer than the stamens—stigma four-cleft—capsule radical, sessile, containing four cells.

The specific name of this very interesting plant was given by Professor Nuttal, in consequence of what he considered the three-lobed form of its petals; this is however so very slight as to be scarcely observable, and therefore perhaps ought not to be considered a specific distinction. It was discovered by the Professor in the Arkansas country, in 1819, and seeds were afterwards brought by that indefatigable traveller and naturalist, Mr. D. Douglas, from North America, in 1824. This plant, which has a succession of flowers throughout the Summer, is extremely liable to decay, if not kept dry in the Winter; but it may be raised from seed, or by parting the roots in Autumn, and keeping them in a frame, in pots of light dry soil, giving them very little or no water until the roots begin to shoot in the Spring. This is the best method of increasing the Œ. cespitosa, a most lovely plant, but extremely difficult to propagate. There are numerous species and varieties of this very interesting genus: some of the most beautiful are—

Œ. frutiosa.	Œ. glauca.
— speciosa.	— grandiflora.
— acaulis.	— amæna.
— rosea.	— tenella.
— pallida.	— viminea.

Plate 23. *Clarkia Pulchella.*

Drawn from Nature by M.R. *Engraved by R. Havell Jun[r.]*

C L A R K I A pulchella.

Pretty Clarkia.

Class and Order.—Tetrandria Monogynia.

Syn. Clarkia pulchella. *Pursh. Fl. N. A., vol.* i. *p.* 260. *Bot. Reg., pl.* 1100.

Plant annual—stem erect, branching—leaves linear, lanceolate, sessile, smooth—peduncles short—flowers growing from the axils of the leaves, solitary—calyx one segment, lanceolate, keeled—corolla beautiful purple pink—petals four, trilobed, obtuse, horned at the base—stamens four—anthers involute—style longer than the stamens—stigma divided into four parts—capsule oblong, grooved.

This very beautiful and singular annual was named by Pursh, in honour of Captain Clark, the companion of Captain Lewis, whose interesting travels across the continent of North America are so well known. It was found by Mr. Douglas, in the countries around the Columbia river, and brought by him into this country, to the Horticultural Society. The plant is hardy; but to facilitate its bloom, the seeds should be sown in a hotbed early in the Spring, and when the plants have acquired sufficient strength they may be removed to the borders, where they will continue to flower until destroyed by frost. This is the only species known of this genus.

Pl. 23.

Plate 24. Potentilla Nipalensis.

Drawn from Nature by M.R.

Engraved by R. Havell Jun.

POTENTILLA Nipalensis.

Nipal Potentilla.

Class and Order.—Icosandria Polygynia.

Syn. Potentilla Nipalensis. *Hooker's Exotic Flora, vol. ii., pl. 88.*

Root fibrous—stem erect, branching—radical leaves, quinate—leaflets obovate, lanceolate, serrate—stipules large, broad, lanceolate—flowers terminal, on long peduncles—calyx double—five outer segments small, five inner somewhat larger—corolla five petals, emarginate, beautiful rose colour, darker at the base—stamens numerous—styles many—whole plant, hairy.

For this beautiful species of Potentilla we are indebted to the celebrated Dr. Wallich, of the Botanic Garden, Calcutta, who discovered it in Nipal, and sent seeds of it to this country. It is now becoming generally known, and is a great acquisition to our gardens, both for the beauty of its flower and continuing so long in blossom. A light loam suits it best; and when it likes the situation it will sow itself, and is therefore easily propagated. The genus Potentilla is not a showy one, but there are several pretty species:—

P. atrosanguinea.	P. lupinaster.
— clusiana.	— nivea.
— hirta.	— pedata.

AUTUMN.

Though Summer with her fervid ray,
No longer leads the lengthened day,
Though Autumn with her sober tread
Appears upon the russet mead,
For her shall Flora form her wreath,
And still around her fragrance breathe;
Shall still with beauty deck the plain,
Nor cease midst darker hours to reign.

Plate 33. *Eschscholtzia Californica.*

Drawn from Nature by M.R. Junr.

Engraved by R. Havell

ESCHSCHOLTZIA Californica.

Californian Eschscholtzia.

Class and Order.—POLYANDRIA TETRAGYNIA.

Syn. Eschscholtzia Californica. *Bot. Reg. pl.* 1168.

Root fusiform—stem branching, growing to the height of one foot or more—leaves glaucous, tri-pinnatifid, segments acute—flowers terminal, on long peduncles—Calyx formed like the Calyptra of a Moss, which falls off previous to the expansion of the flower—petals four—large, spreading, slightly striated, narrower at the base, margins undulate, of a brilliant yellow, which increases to an orange in the centre of the flower—stamens numerous, filaments very short, anthers long, acute—stigmas four—seed vessel subulate.

Fig. 1. represents the seed pod. Fig. 2. the curiously formed Calyx.

This elegant flower was originally discovered by Mr. Menzies, during the expedition of Vancouver, in the year 1792, on the coast of California. It has been named by Chamisso after Dr. Eschscholtz, a companion of Kotzebue, in his voyage round the world, and was sent to the Hort. Soc., by Mr. Douglas, in 1826, who found it on the N. W. coast of America. It promises to be a very desirable and beautiful addition to our catalogue of herbaceous plants, flowering abundantly all thro' the summer 'till destroyed by frost. It may be propagated either by seeds, which should be sown in a hot-bed early in the spring, or by parting the roots in autumn, and grows best in a pure air, and a light, or sandy soil.

Pl. 33.

Plate 34. Catananche Cœrulea.

Drawn from Nature by M.R.

Junr. **Engraved by R. Havell**

CATANANCHE cœrulea.

Blue Catananche.

Class and Order.—Syngenesia Polygamia Æqualis.

Syn. Catananche Cœrulea. *Curtis Bot. Mag. pl.* 293.

Root fibrous—Stem radical, branching—growing to the height of two feet—Radical leaves, long, lanceolate, margins deeply toothed—back of the leaf downy, and strongly nerved—Cauline leaves, sessile, linear, acute. Flowers terminal on very long peduncles on which are scattered membranaceous bracteas—Calyx imbricate, squamose, membranaceous, striate—Corolla blue—Florets ligulate, apex three toothed, purple at the base, fertile—Stamens five, Anthers united—style one, stigma bifid.

There are only two species known of this genus, the one here figured is a native of the South of Europe, and is said to have been cultivated by Parkinson as far back as the year 1640, it is however by no means a common plant, owing perhaps to the difficulty of keeping it through the winter, when it is very apt to be destroyed by frost; it is easily raised from seeds which may be sown in the autumn, and if protected during the winter, will make strong plants to flower through the ensuing summer, continuing in beauty until the approach of winter—it likes a dry, sandy soil, and will not bear frequent removal,—the other species, Catananche lutea, is an annual not deserving of cultivation.

Pl. 34.

Plate 35. *Coreopsis Grandiflora.*

Drawn from Nature by M.R.

Engraved by R. Havell Junr·

COREOPSIS Grandiflora.

Large flowered Coreopsis.

Class and Order.—Syngenesia Polygamia Frustranea.

Syn. Coreopsis Grandiflora. *Sweet's B. F. G. Vol. 2. pl.* 175.

Root fibrous, creeping—Stem, tall, erect, branched. Leaves on short petioles ternate, leaflets lanceolate, acute—cauline leaves becoming more linear. Flowers large, terminal, on long, slender peduncles—Calyx double, exterior segments green, lanceolate acute; interior segments brown, membranaceous—Corolla bright yellow, radiated florets barren, dentate; florets of the disk fertile.

This fine species is so similar to C. Lanceolata, that it is only to be distinguished by the leaf, the flowers being alike in form and color, though perhaps a little larger in C. grandiflora—it was found by Professor Nuttall in the Arkansas, and was sent by him to Mr. Barclay about the year 1826; it is therefore from its late introduction yet rare in our collections, it promises to be of easy cultivation, its creeping roots throwing up a plentiful supply of young plants from which it may easily be propagated—a little protection in the winter may perhaps be desirable.

Amongst the most beautiful species of this genus are

- C. lanceolata
- — tinctoria.
- — verticillata.
- — tenuifolia.

Plate 36. *Georgina Coccinea.*
Drawn from Nature by M.R.
Engraved by R. Havell Junr.

GEORGINA coccinea.

Scarlet flowered Georgina.

Class and Order.—Syngenesia Polygamia Superflua.

Syn. Georgina Coccinea *Wildenow Enum. Plant. Vol. 2. p. 338.*

Dahlia Coccinea. *Curt. Bot. Mag. pl. 762.*

Root tuberous—stem upright, branched, growing from three to five feet high. Leaves pinnate, lower leaves sometimes bi-pinnate, leaflets serrate—flowers terminal, on long purple peduncles—calyx double, exterior segments somewhat reflexed, obtuse—corolla bright scarlet—radiated florets ovate, obtuse, furnished with a style only—florets of the disk, containing both stamens and pistils.

This distinct species, which is perhaps one of the most beautiful of the genus is readily distinguished by its small flower and foliage—it is a native of Mexico, and previous to its introduction to this country, by Mr. Fraser, in 1803, was cultivated in France,—endless varieties of this genus are constantly raised from seed, and by other means, and there is no flower to which we are so much indebted for ornamenting our gardens in the Autumn—the cultivation of this plant is so easy, and now so well known that little requires to be said on this point. Particular care, however, must be taken to keep the roots from frost; a poor soil will cause a smaller growth, and produce more flowers. The name Georgina was given to this genus by Wildenow, in honor of G. Georgi, a Russian Botanist, and as it is considered by the Continental and many English Botanists, to be the most correct, it has been here adopted, instead of Dahlia, a name very similar to that of another genus (Dalea) called after Dale the friend of Ray;[1] some of the most beautiful double Georginas are varieties of the Sambucifolia.

G. frustranea.   G. atro purpurea.
— superflua.   — rubra.
— alba.   — atro-rubra.
— flava.   — fulgens.

— purpurea.   — crocea.

[1] See Bot. Mag. page 762, and Sweets British Flower Garden, page 282. Pl. 36.

Plate 37. *Rudbeckia hirta.*
Drawn from Nature by M.R.

Junr. *Engraved by R. Havell*

RUDBECKIA hirta.

Hairy Rudbeckia.

Class and Order.—Syngenesia Polygamia Frustranea.

Syn. Rudbeckia hirta. *Pursh. Flo. N. A. page* 574.

Root Fibrous—stem erect, branched, grooved. Radical leaves broad, lanceolate, cauline leaves sessile, unequal, margins undulate peduncles one flowered, terminal—calyx many segments, lanceolate, obtuse—corolla bright yellow—radiated florets, linear, lanceolate recurved, barren—florets of the disk fertile—whole plant hairy.

The genus Rudbeckia (called after Professor Rudbeck of Upsal who died in 1702) is a very ornamental one, its different species making a gay appearance in the Autumn. R. hirta is perhaps one of the most desirable, from its moderate size, seldom growing higher than two feet—it was introduced about the year 1714, it is a native of N. America, and is found on the mountains from Virginia to Florida—it likes a light rich soil, and is propagated by parting the roots, which should be done in the spring, as it flowers so late in Autumn as to prevent the removal in sufficient time for the plants to be well established before winter—it is rather tender, sometimes being destroyed by too much wet. The following are pleasing species:—

- R. purpurea.
- — fulgida.
- — columnaris.
- — speciosa.
- — pinnata.

Plate 38. *Scabiosa Caucasea.*
Drawn from Nature by M.R.

Engraved by R. Havell Junr·

SCABIOSA Caucasea.

Caucasean Scabious.

Class and Order.—TETRANDRIA MONOGYNIA.

Syn. Scabiosa Caucasea. *Curt. Bot. Mag. pl. 886.*

Root fibrous—stem erect, rising to the height of two feet or more—radical leaves on long channelled footstalks, lanceolate, acute, margins undulate, cauline leaves, connate, pinnatifid—peduncles one flowered, flowers terminal—involucre from eight to ten segments, lanceolate, acute—corolla delicate purple, segments trilobed, lobes obtuse, margins undulate, florets of the disk tubular, margins five-cleft—Calyx double—stamens four, anthers oblong, of a bright red, style longer than the stamens; stigma globose; germen downy.

This is perhaps the most beautiful species of the genus; and a highly ornamental plant in the Autumnal months, during which time it continues long in beauty, it is a native of Mount Caucasus, and according to the Bot. Mag. p. 886, was raised by Messrs. Loddiges from seeds received by them about the year 1803—a light soil suits it best, and it may be increased by parting its roots in the spring—it is quite hardy.

The genus Scabiosa is not a favorite one for a flower garden, though a few species may deserve a place in our collections—some of the most desirable are

        S. alpina.
        — tatarica.
        — atropurpurea.
        — lœvigata.

Plate 39. *Lobelia fulgens.*
Drawn from Nature by M.R. Junr
Engraved by R. Havell

LOBELIA fulgens.

Refulgent Lobelia.

Class and Order.—Pentandria Monogynia.

Syn. Lobelia fulgens. *Bot. Rep. pl.* 659.

Root fibrous—stem erect, leafy, occasionally drooping at the summit, downy. Leaves alternate sessile, broad lanceolate, undulate, denticulate near the point, veined, becoming smaller towards the top of the stem—peduncles very short—calyx five segments, acute, downy—corolla monopetalous, very brilliant scarlet—tube oblong, inflated at the base, segments five, three lower ones, oblong, lanceolate, acute; two upper, small, linear, acute, recurved—stamens five—anthers oblong, style filiform—stigma compressed.

This brilliant ornament to the flower garden is a native of Mexico, and was raised from seeds sent by Humboldt and Bonpland, to this country, about the year 1809—it is a plant of easy cultivation, and is readily increased by parting the roots in Spring—it is hardy, but in the winter requires to be kept dry, as it is liable to decay from too much moisture, it is therefore the safest plan to put a few plants in a frame, divide them, and plant them about April, in a stiff soil, and moist situation, where they will flourish exceedingly, and make a splendid appearance until destroyed by frost—This species differs little from L. Splendens, which has its foliage more tinged with red and is devoid of that pubescence which distinguishes L. fulgens.

There are several beautiful species of this genus, but few are hardy, those most desirable for a flower garden are

- L. splendens.
- — cardinalis.
- — amæna.
- — tupa.

Plate 40. *Aster Amellus.*

Drawn from Nature by M.R.　　　*Engraved by R. Havell Jun[r.]*

A S T E R amellus.

Italian aster.

―――◆―――

Class and Order.—Syngenesia Polygamia Superflua.

Syn. Aster Amellus. *Hortus Kewensis, vol.* 5, *page* 54.

Root fibrous—stem erect, branched, sometimes two feet high—leaves sessile, alternate, ovate lanceolate, obtuse—margins undulate. Flowers purple, corymbose, on short peduncles; calyx imbricated—radiated florets, linear, obtuse, furnished with a style only—florets of the disk fertile containing both stamens and pistils.

―――◆―――

Few autumnal plants are more deserving of cultivation than the Aster Amellus—the beauty of the flower, its moderately low growth, and late flowering, rendering it a valuable plant for the season, and perhaps preferable to any of the genus—it is a native of the South of Europe, and was cultivated in this country, as long since as 1596, by Gerard, it will grow in any soil or situation, and flowers from September until destroyed by severe frost—it may be increased by dividing the roots, which according to Miller should not be moved oftener than every third year.

The genus aster is a very numerous one, and affords some ornamental species

   A. alpina.   A. nova angliæ.
   — blandus.   — spectabilis.
   — elegans.   — pulcherrimus.
   — grandiflorus.

Pl. 40.

WINTER.

―――◆―――

―— The fairer forms
That cultivation glories in, are His,
He sets the bright procession on its way,
And marshalls all the order of the Year;
He marks the bounds that Winter may not pass,
And blunts his pointed fury: in its case

Russet and rude folds up the tender germ
Uninjured, with inimitable art,
And ere one flowery season fades and dies,
Designs the blooming wonders of the next.
                                        Cowper.

Plate 49. Semi-Double quilled pink Chrysanthemum.

Drawn from Nature by M.R.

Engraved by R. Havell Jun[r.]

CHRYSANTHEMUM indicum var.

Semi double quill'd pink Chrysanthemum.

Class and Order.—Syngensia, Polygamia, Superflua.

Syn. Semi double quill'd pink Chrysanthemum. *Hort. Soc. Trans. Vol. 5. p. 422.*

Stem tall, erect, leafy, branching—lower leaves large, bi-pinnatifid, lobes deeply indented—becoming smaller as they approach the flower—flower terminal slightly pendant—calyx squamose—florets quill'd of a beautiful pale pink, shaded off to white—disc yellow—large.

The first introduction of the Chinese Chrysanthemums into this country, was about the year 1764;—the beautiful varieties now seen in our gardens, became known at a much more recent period, and from the great facility that attends their cultivation, and their very desirable season of flowering, they are universal favorites;—new varieties are frequently imported, the only means we possess of obtaining them, as we are ignorant of the mode adopted by the Chinese for their increase; and we are led to suppose that we do not yet possess some of their finest kinds:—most of the varieties will grow well out of doors, and if trained against a south wall, with a little protection to shield the flowers from inclement weather, will make a beautiful and gay appearance in the months of November and December. The Chrysanthemums are increased either by cuttings or suckers taken from the parent plant in the spring;—the var. here figured is a very beautiful one, and blossoms rather early and freely—the flowers have a deeper color when grown out of doors, and the plant altogether acquires more strength;—in a green-house this var. is apt to grow weak and tall.

Pl. 49.

Plate 50. *Superb White Chrysanthemum.*
Early Crimson.

Drawn from Nature by M.R. Junr. *Engraved by R. Havell*

CHRYSANTHEMUM indicum var.

Superb White Chrysanthemum.

Class and Order.—Syngensia, Polygamia, Superflua.

Syn. Superb White Chrysanthemum. *Hort. Soc. Trans. Vol.* 5. *p.* 420.

Stem erect, leafy, branching—leaves bi-pinnatifid, lobes deeply indented,—flower terminal, drooping, white, tinged with yellow towards the centre—calyx squamose, obtuse, florets ligulate, outside florets occasionally quill'd—apex entire.

This variety is a very desirable one for growing out of doors, from its long continuance in bloom, and the flowers being so very large and fine—the foilage is luxuriant, and if the plant be trained against a wall, it will grow very tall, and make a beautiful appearance until a late season;—the Chrysanthemums like a strong soil.

CHRYSANTHEMUM indicum var.

Early Crimson Chrysanthemum.

Class and Order.—Syngensia, Polygamia, Superflua.

Syn. Early Crimson Chrysanthemum. *Hort. Soc. Trans. Vol.* 5, *p.* 155.

Stem erect, leafy, much branched—leaves bi-pinnatifid, lobes very deeply indented—flowers pendant—growing in clusters, semi-double, of a fine crimson—florets ligulate, emarginate—disc small.

This is a newer var. than either the superb white, or quill'd pink; the plant grows low, and rather bushy, and makes a very brilliant appearance when in full flower—the varieties of Chrysanthemum Indicum are so endless, that is difficult to make a selection; some of the most beautiful and latest imported are the following:—

Purple.	Blush Ranunculus flowered.
Quill'd white.	Tasselled lilac.
Tasselled white.	Two colored red.
Sulphur yellow.	Starry pink.
Golden yellow.	Two colored incurved.
Buff or orange.	Golden Lotus flowered.
Quill'd flamed yellow.	Brown lilac.
Curled lilac.	Early blush.
Pale pink.	Paper white.
Parks' small yellow.	Changeable pale buff.

Pl. 50.

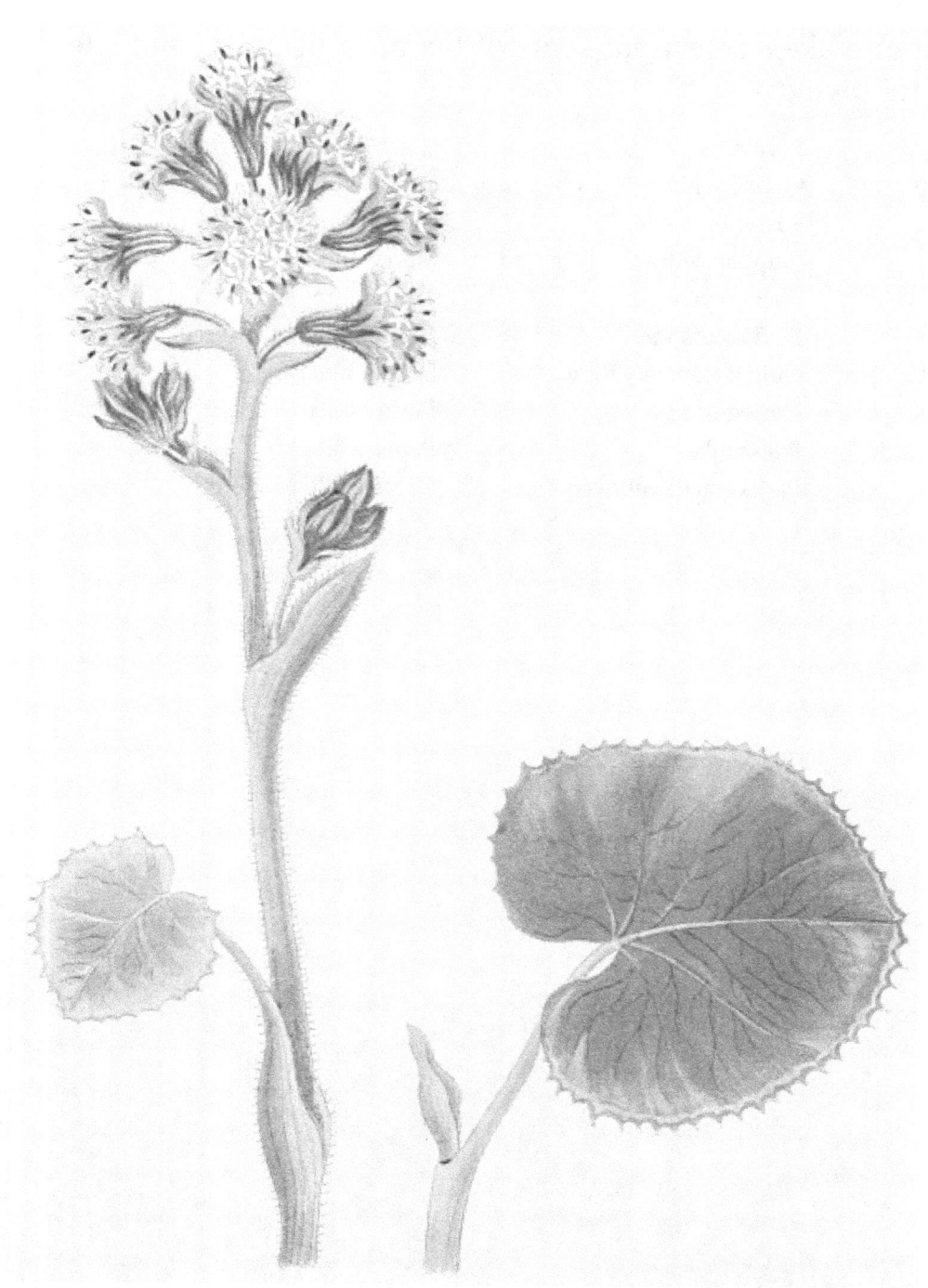

Plate 51. Tussilago fragrans.
Drawn from Nature by M.R.

Engraved by R. Havell Jun.

TUSSILAGO fragrans.

Fragrant Coltsfoot.

Class and Order.—Syngensia, Polygamia, Superflua.

Syn. Tussilago Fragrans. *Curt. Bot. Mag. pl.* 1388.

Root creeping, fleshy—scape about eight inches high, woolly, appearing before the leaves—leaves radical, large, cordate, margins crenate—young leaves covered with a deciduous down, cauline leaves cordate, sheathing the stem—peduncles rising from concave bracteas—calyx many segments, lanceolate, acute, tinged with brown—radiated florets ligulate, pink, florets of the disk, five segments, white—style projecting, stigma dark purple.

This plant possesses little beauty to recommend it to our notice, but its delightful fragrance, which strongly resembles the Heliotropium Peruvianum, renders it an acceptable addition to our small stock of winter flowers. It is a native of Italy, and was introduced into this country by Messrs. Lee and Kennedy, in 1806. Though frequently treated as a greenhouse or frame-plant, it is perfectly hardy, and if grown in a moist situation, it will spread so rapidly as to become troublesome; the best plan therefore is to confine it in a pot, and plunge it in common garden soil, where it will flower about December or January, without the least protection.

This is the only species suitable for a flower garden.

Pl. 51.

Plate 52. *Helleborus niger.*
Drawn from Nature by M.R.

Engraved by R. Havell Junr.

HELLEBORUS niger.

Black Hellebore or Christmas Rose.

Class and Order.—POLYANDRIA POLYGYNIA.

Syn. Helleborus niger. *Curt. Bot. Mag. pl. 8.*

Root tuberous—leaves radical, on long channelled petioles, pedate, lobes oblong, margins serrate near the apex—scape radical, simple,—flower terminal—calyx none—bracteas immediately under the flower, two, sessile—corolla white, slightly tinged with pale pink and yellowish green,—petals five, large, orbicular, margins undulate—nectaries green, tubular—stamens numerous—anthers compressed—styles many.

There are few flowers more welcome to us than the Helleborus niger, which enlivens our gardens in the dreary months of December and January. It is a native of the mountains of Austria, and was introduced into this country about the year 1596, by Mr. John Gerard; it derives its name from the dark color of its roots, and the common appellation of the Christmas Rose, arises from the peculiar season of its flowering; being an alpine plant it delights in a pure air, and it grows best in a moist situation and strong loamy soil: it may be covered with a hand-glass when coming into bloom, as the beauty of the flower is liable to be destroyed by the severity of the weather. Considerable medicinal properties were ascribed to this plant by the ancients, but it is now seldom used. There are several other species, but only two of these are generally cultivated—the first mentioned is a British plant.

> H. viridis.
> — lividus.

Plate 53. *Eranthis hyemalis.*
Drawn from Nature by M.R.
Engraved by R. Havell Jun[r.]

ERANTHIS hyemalis

Winter Aconite.

Class and Order.—POLYANDRIA POLYGYNIA.

Syn. Eranthis hyemalis. *Salisbury, Lin. Soc. Trans. Vol. 8. p.* 303.

Helleborus hyemalis. *Curt. Bot. Mag. Vol. 1. p.* 3.

Root tuberous—leaves radical, on long petioles, radiated, palmate, lobes generally trifid—scape radical, one flowered—involucrum sessile, lobed, becoming larger when the flower decays—corolla yellow—petals six, or sometimes more, obovate, nectaries tubular, stamens from twenty to thirty—anthers compressed—styles many.

The genus Eranthis, which was established by Salisbury, differs from Helleborus in the number of its petals and stamens, the latter in Eranthis are from twenty to thirty, in Helleborus, from thirty to sixty; the seed in the former genus being in one series, the latter in two series, the difference of habit, &c., altogether forming good grounds for making them separate genera. This pretty species which flowers about January is a native of France, Switzerland, and Austria, and was cultivated in our gardens as long since as 1596;—it grows best in a light loam mixed with bog, and is propagated by offsets. There is another species Eranthis Siberica.

Pl. 53.

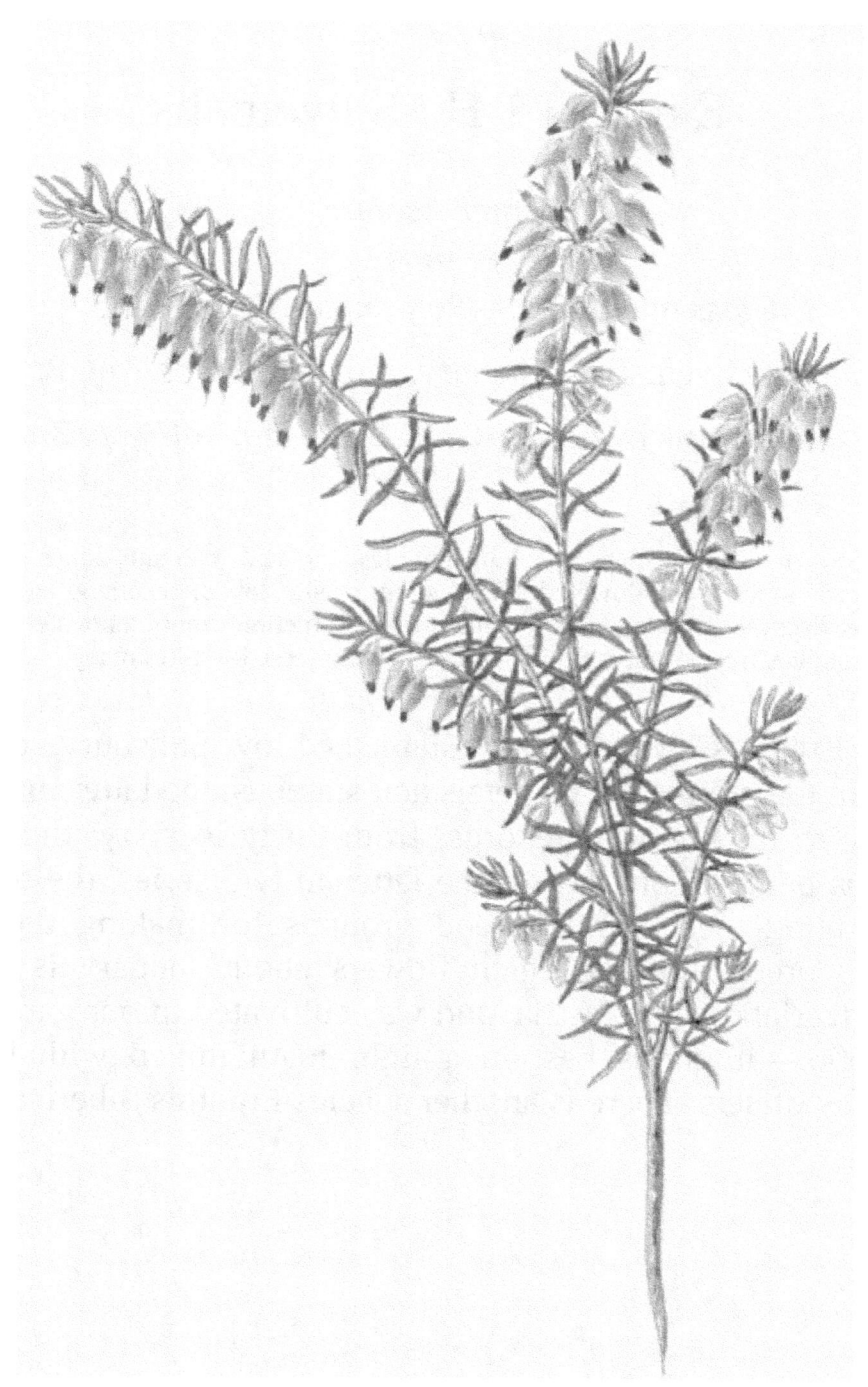

Plate 54. *Erica carnea.*

Drawn from Nature by M.R.   *Engraved by R. Havell Junr·*

ERICA carnea.

Flesh colored, early Flowering Heath.

Class and Order.—Octandria Monogynia.

Syn. Erica carnea.	*Jacquin's Flo. Austr. Vol.* 1. *tab.* 32.
Erica carnea.	*Loddige's Bot. Cab. p.* 1452.
Erica herbacea.	*Curt. Bot. Mag. pl.* 11.

Root fibrous—stem branching upon the ground, leaves small, linear, sessile—flowers pendulous, on very short peduncles—calyx four segments, linear acute—corolla campanulate, pale pink, margin four cleft—stamens eight fixed to the receptacle, anthers bifid, projecting, dark purple—style declining, longer than the stamens.

This pretty little plant would be acceptable to us at any season of the year, but is peculiarly so in the dreary one in which its beautiful pink blossoms appear, frequently peeping above the snow. The flowers are formed in the autumn, but do not come to maturity until the following December or January, when (if planted in a bog border with a south aspect) it will make a beautiful appearance for a length of time. It is a native of the Alps and mountainous parts of Germany, and was introduced into this country about the year 1763; the general method of increasing this plant is by cuttings or layers,—there are other species of hardy heaths which are well worth cultivating. The three last mentioned are natives of Britain.

E. Mediterranea.	E. tetralia.
— ciliaris.	— vagans.
— carnea var.	— stricta.
— Australis.	

Pl. 54.

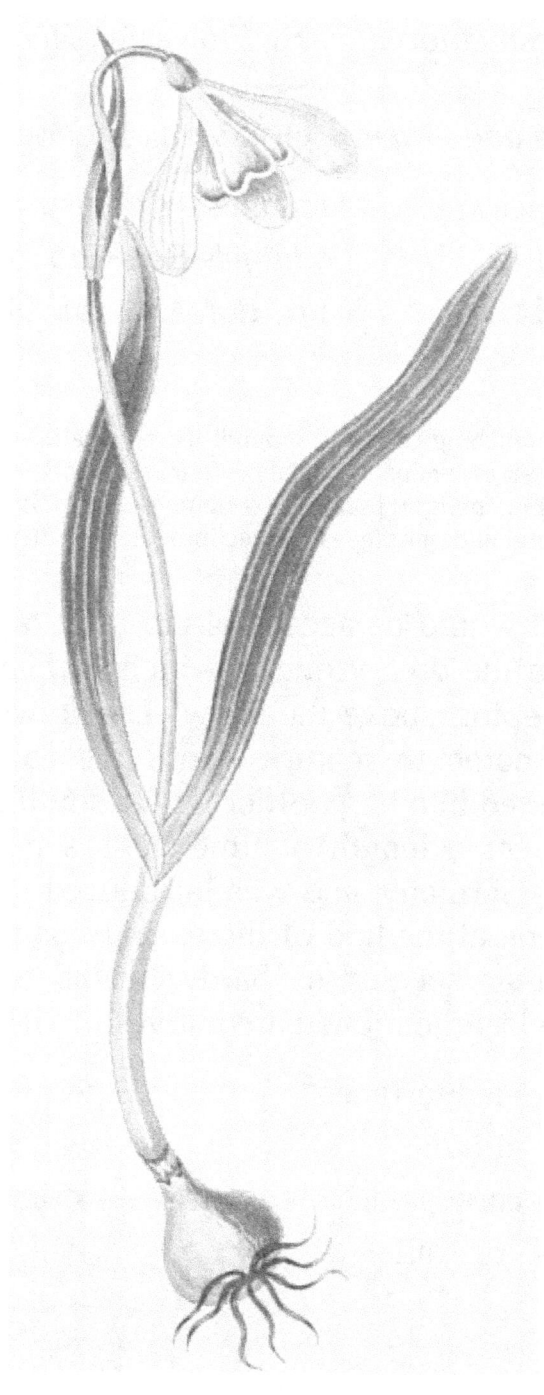

Plate 55. Galanthus Nivalis.

Drawn from Nature by M.R.   *Engraved by R. Havell Jun[r.]*

G A L A N T H U S nivalis.

Common Snowdrop.

Class and Order.—HEXANDRIA MONOGYNIA.

Syn. Galanthus nivalis. *English Bot. pl.* 19.

Root bulbous.—Scape from three to five inches high, one flowered. Leaves two, broadly linear, obtuse, glaucous green, sheathing the lower part of the stem.—Flower drooping, bursting from a sheath, lanceolate.—Corolla white, petals three, oblong, obtuse—nectaries three emarginate, beautifully tipped with green—stamens six, anthers subulate—style one, stigma simple.

This beautiful flower so well known, and so peculiarly interesting from its modest simplicity, hardly requires a description of its treatment or mode of growth. It is a native of England, having been found in many places remote from cultivation, and will grow in any soil or situation.—A double var. is frequently met with in our gardens, there is also another species G. plicatus, a native of Caucasus.

Pl. 55.

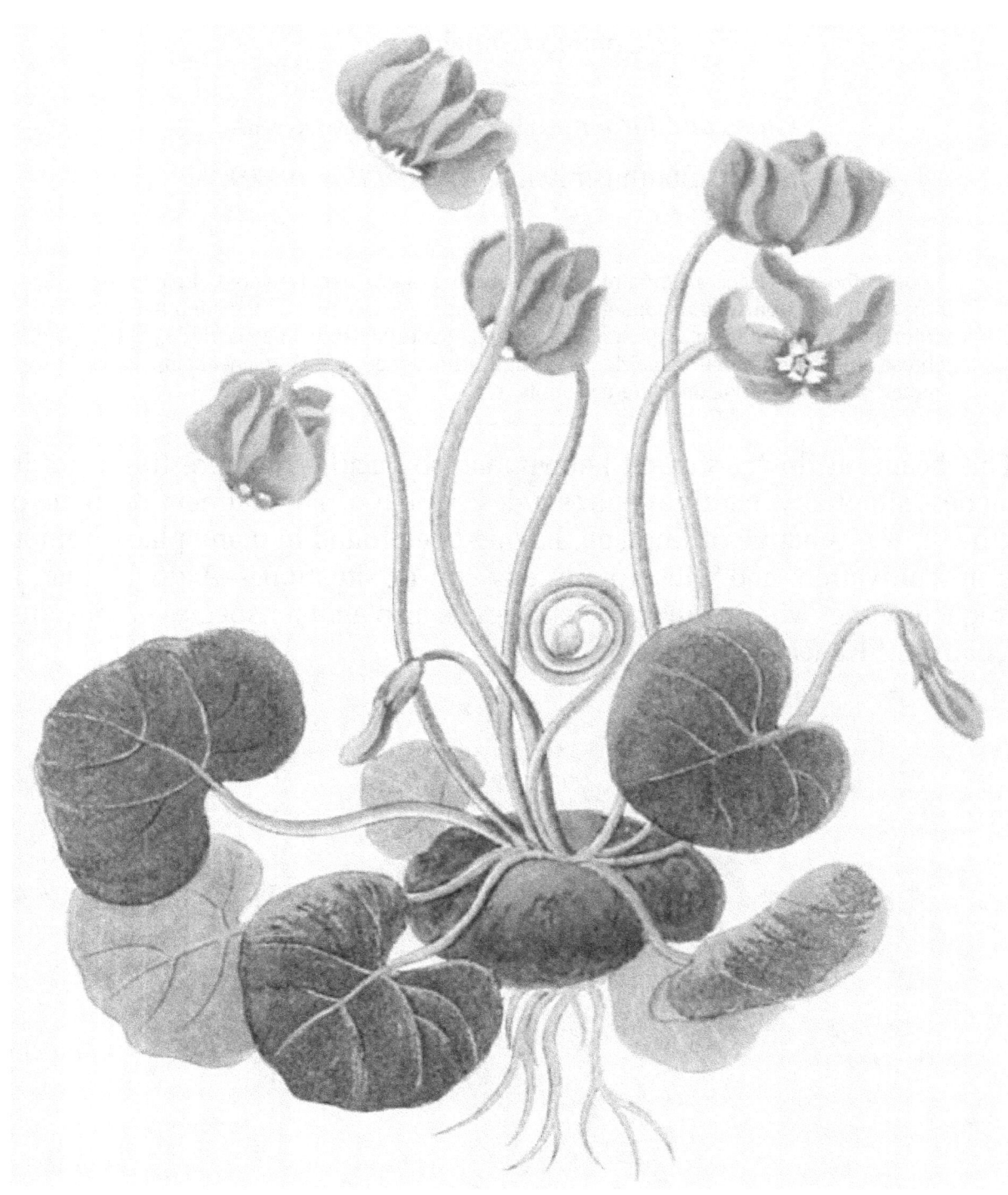

Plate 9. Cyclamen Coum.

Drawn from Nature by M.R.

Engraved by R. Havell Jun[r.]

CYCLAMEN Coum.

Round leaved Cyclamen.

Class and Order.—Pentandria Monogynia.

| Syn. Cyclamen Coum. | *Cur. Bot. Mag. pl.* 4. |
| — Cyclamen Coum. | *Hor. Kew.* 1 *vol. p.* 311. |

Root bulbous, orbicular, compressed. Leaves radical, on rather long purplish petioles, orbicular, cordate, upper side dark green, red underneath—stem radical, three or four inches high, flower terminal, drooping—calyx five segments acute—petals five, reflexed, ovate, margins undulate, dark pink, marked with red at the base, which is shaded off to a pure white, stamens five enclosed in the tube of the corolla, style longer than the stamens, stigma acute.

This pretty plant which is one of the earliest of our Spring bulbs, is a native of the south of Europe, and has been known since the year 1596, when it was cultivated by Mr. John Gerard. It is very hardy, though generally treated as a green-house or frame plant, and if grown in a sheltered situation in a mixture of bog earth, and rich loam, it will flower abundantly, and make a beautiful appearance about February, particularly if covered with a hand-glass to protect the flowers from the inclemency of the weather.

This plant is easily raised from seed, which is produced in abundance. After the petals decay the germen becomes enlarged, and the foot stalk enclosing it in the centre, twists in the form of a screw, until it reaches the ground, when the seed-vessel bursts and deposits the seed, a beautiful provision of nature for propagating the species—the seeds thus sown, will require a little more soil, and the protection of a hand-glass during the Winter, when if not destroyed by frost, the plants will generally flower the following Summer—the other hardy species are

C. hederæfolium.
———— var.
— europæum.

Pl. 9.

Plate 10. Hyoscyamus Orientalis.
Drawn from Nature by M.R.

Engraved by R. Havell Jun.

HYOSCYAMUS Orientalis.

Oriental Hyoscyamus.

Class and Order.—Pentandria Monogynia.

Syn. Hyoscyamus Orientalis.	*Beburstein Fl. Taur. Cauc. vol. 1. p. 164.*
— Hyoscyamus Orientalis.	*Curt. Bot. Mag. pl. 2414.*

Root tuberous—stem erect, growing to the height of one foot or more—leaves on rather long petioles, broadly lanceolate, spreading, margins undulate, of a dull green, strongly veined with red—under side reddish in the young leaves—flowers thyrsiform—on short pedicels—calyx campanulate, margin five cleft, segments acute, tinged with purple—corolla lilac, funnel shaped, limb spreading, five cleft—stamens five, inclined, shorter than the style—stigma clavate—whole plant covered with a whitish pubescence which it nearly loses in more advanced growth.

The genus Hyoscyamus is, perhaps, more remarkable for its medicinal properties than for its beauty, though this species is certainly a handsome plant and as yet rarely met with:—it is of later introduction than Hyoscyamus Physaloides, which has a darker flower, the leaves perfectly smooth, and the plant altogether is of smaller growth. H. Orientalis is a native of Iberia, a country between the Black and Caspian Seas, and was first introduced into this country from seeds sent to Mr. John Hunneman, about the year 1821; it is perfectly hardy, likes a rich soil, and may be increased by parting the roots or by seed; flowers as early as March. There is only another species besides the two mentioned, deserving of cultivation in a flower garden, which is H. Scopoli.

Pl. 10.

Plate 11. *Orobus Vernus.*
Drawn from Nature by M.R.

Junr.   *Engraved by R. Havell*

OROBUS Vernus.

Spring Orobus.

Class and Order.—DIADELPHIA DECANDRIA.

Syn. Orobus Vernus.	*Car. Bot. Mag. pl.* 521.
— Orobus Vernus.	*Hor. Kew. vol.* 3. *p.* 38.

Root fibrous—stem erect, branching, one foot or more in height—stipules large, sagittate, auriculate—leaves pinnate—leaflets ovate, acute—peduncles long, axillary—pedicels very short—calyx five cleft, base obtuse, tinted with red—flower papilionaceous—vexillum pink, broadly ovate, margin undulate—alæ blue, obtuse; carina white—stamens ten, united by their filaments into two parcels, nine in one set, with a single one separate—style one.

The Orobus vernus is a most valuable Spring flower, and is one of the earliest of our herbaceous plants;—it is a native of the middle and south of Europe, and was first introduced into this country about the year 1629;—a light soil suits it best, though being very hardy it will flourish in any situation, and considering the facility with which it is cultivated, it is surprizing it is not more common;—it flowers in March, and is increased by dividing the roots or by seed—some of the most desirable species are

O. niger.	albus.
— varius.	tuberosus.
— lathyroides.	variegatus.
— luteus.	ochroleucus.

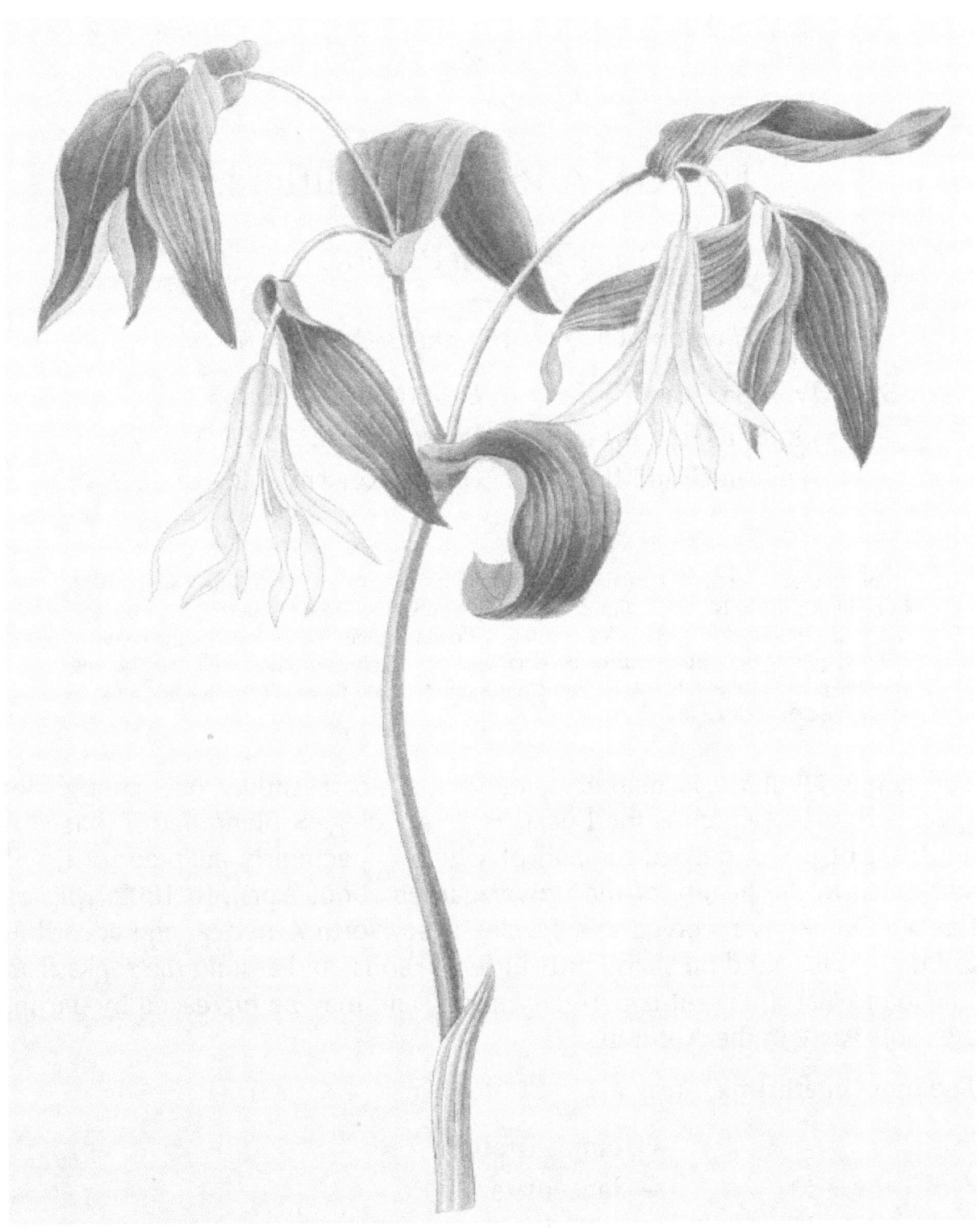

Plate 12. *Uvularia Grandiflora.*
Drawn from Nature by M.R.

Junr. *Engraved by R. Havell*

UVULARIA Grandiflora.

Large flowered Uvularia.

Class and Order.—HEXANDRIA MONOGYNIA.

Syn. Uvularia Grandiflora.	*Exotic Botany, Tab.* 51.
— Uvularia Grandiflora.	*Pursh Flo. N. A. Vol.* 1. *p.* 231.
— Uvularia Grandiflora.	*Hortus Kewensis,* 2. *Vol. p.* 247.

Root tuberous—stem a foot or more in height, radical, erect, sheathed at the base, branching towards the summit—petioles flexuose—leaves perfoliate, broadly lanceolate, undulate—peduncles axillary—flowers pendulous—calyx none—corolla yellow, petals six, linear, tortuose—stamens six, filaments short—anthers oblong, linear—germen obovate—style one, stigma divided into three parts—nectary a cavity at the base of each petal.

The genus Uvularia is neither a numerous, nor a showy one, though the species figured (which is the finest) is a very elegant plant, and if placed in the front of a bog border, the soil of which is peculiarly adapted to it, will add much to the beauty of the flower garden about April. In 1802, Messrs. Lee and Kennedy received this species from North America, and according to Pursh, it is found on shady hills in fertile soils, and among the rocks from Canada to Carolina;—it is perfectly hardy, and may be increased by parting the roots early in the Autumn.

The most interesting, are

> U. amplexifolia.
> — lanceolata.
> — perfoliata.
> — sessilifolia.

Plate 13. *Gentiana Verna.*

Drawn from Nature by M.R. Junr.

Engraved by R. Havell

GENTIANA verna.

Spring Gentian.

Class and Order.—Pentandria Digynia.

Syn. Gentiana verna.	*Eng. Bot. pl.* 493.
— Gentiana verna.	*Curt. Bot. Mag. pl.* 491.

Root fibrous, creeping—stem procumbent, leafy,—leaves sessile, oval, acute, opposite, clustered near the root—flowers terminal—calyx five cleft, acute—corolla brilliant blue, monopetalous, tube long, limb spreading, divided into five segments, obtuse, undulate, fringed between the segments—stamens five, enclosed in the tube of the corolla—style simple, stigmas two, so closely situated as to give the appearance of a small white circle in the centre of the flower.

This beautiful little plant is well ascertained to be a native of England and Ireland. According to English Botany, p. 49—it was first gathered in Teesdale Forest, Durham, where it is still obtained for the purposes of sale in London, and other places;—it is also a native of the Alps of Switzerland, where we are told the large patches of it produce a brilliant and striking effect:—it is perfectly hardy, but requires a pure air, and succeeds best in bog-soil—from its low growth and general habit, it is well adapted to ornament rock work, and from the shelter there afforded, it will begin to flower as early as March, and continue in beauty some time—it may be increased by parting the roots early in the Autumn:—the Gentiana lutea, is celebrated for its medicinal properties, and is a handsome herbaceous plant; the other desirable species are

G. crinita.	purpurea.
— asclepedia.	septemfida.
— saponaria.	acaulis.
— alpina.	pneunomanthe.

Plate 14. *Soldanella Clusii.*

Drawn from Nature by M.R.

Engraved by R. Havell Junr.

SOLDANELLA Clusii.

Clusius's Soldanella.

Class and Order.—PENTANDRIA MONOGYNIA.

| Syn. Soldanella Clusii. | Curt. Bot. Mag. pl. 2163. |
| — Soldanella montana? | Sweet's B. F. G. vol. 1. p. 11. |

Root fibrous—leaves radical, on long petioles, orbicular, cordate, slightly crenate, of a dark green, paler underneath—stem radical, erect, three or four inches high—segments of the involucrum linear—flowers terminal, drooping,—calyx five, segments linear, spreading—corolla purple, monopetalous, campanulate, margin deeply laciniated—stamens five, anthers two lobed—style very long, germen inferior.

The beautiful genus Soldanella is peculiarly adapted to rock work, to which it is a great ornament; the different species are all hardy, but like many alpine plants, require shelter from severe frosts, as a substitute for the snow of their native mountains; this species is found on the mountains of Bohemia, and on the Austrian and Styrian Alps, and was introduced into this country about the year 1816. It grows best in a mixture of peat and sandy loam, and is readily increased by seeds, or by parting the roots; the genus is by no means common, perhaps, from their requiring a very pure air to grow them in perfection; it is the safest plan to keep all alpine plants in a frame during winter, or to cover them with *dry* saw dust, over which may be placed a hand-glass or garden-pot. This species is called after Clusius a celebrated Botanist, it being (according to the Bot. Mag. p. 211.) first described and figured by him. There are two other beautiful species, with smaller flowers, S. alpina, S. minima.

Plate 15. Viola Palmata.

Drawn from Nature by M.R.

Junr.

Engraved by R. Havell

VIOLA palmata.

Palmate leaved Violet.

Class and Order. PENTANDRIA MONOGYNIA.

Syn. Viola palmata.   *Pursh Flo. N. A. vol. i. p. 172.*
— Viola palmata.   *Nuttall's Gen. N. A. vol. i. p. 147.*

Root tuberous—leaves radical, on very long petioles, palmate, lobes deeply dentate—peduncles one flowered, radical, tinged with purple—calyx five segments linear acute—corolla blue lilac, paler on the under side, petals five, broad, obtuse, pencilled at the base with a darker shade, lower part of the middle petal terminating in a spur—stamens five, anthers obtuse—style slender, stigma globose.

The genus Viola is a very numerous one, and can boast of many ornamental species—endless varieties are constantly raised from seed, chiefly of Viola tricolor, though these may at first vary, there is little dependance to be placed on them, as they frequently return to the original species; the number of distinct species, however, is very considerable, amongst which is the one figured; a desirable plant for the front of the borders where it will remain in beauty for a long time—it is a native of North America, and according to the Bot. Cab. p. 1471, grows on dry hills from New England to Virginia. Prof. Nuttall says in his genera of North American plants, vol. i. p. 147, "the genus Viola within its proper limits, is almost equally divided betwixt Europe and the temperate parts of North America." This species was first brought into this country in 1739, though still a scarce plant in our gardens:—the Violas are all well adapted for rock work, and flourish most in a light rich soil and shady situation. They may be increased either by parting the roots, by cuttings, or by seeds; the latter of which are produced in great abundance, and are dispersed by the peculiar elasticity of the capsule, which as soon as its contents are matured, ejects them with considerable force, sometimes to a great distance. Some of the most beautiful species are

V. pedata.	præmorsa.
— altaica.	flabelliflora.
— hederacea.	primulifolia.
— lutea.	grandiflora.
— blanda.	lanceolata.
— uniflora.	Nuttallii.
— odorata.	
— cornuta.	

Pl. 15.

Plate 16. *Trillium Grandiflorum.*

Drawn from Nature by M.R. Junr.

Engraved by R. Havell

TRILLIUM Grandiflorum.

Large flowered Trillium.

Class and Order.—HEXANDRIA TRIGYNIA.

Syn. Trillium Grandiflorum.	*Salisbury Par. Lon. pl. 35.*
— Trillium Grandiflorum.	*Hort. Kew. Vol. 2. p. 329*
— Trillium Grandiflorum.	*Nuttall's gen. N. A. Vol. 1. p. 239.*

Root tuberous, stem radical, simple, eight to ten inches high,—leaves three, sessile, large, spreading, oval shaped, obtuse, margins undulate—peduncle short—flower terminal, drooping—calyx three segments, lanceolate, acute—corolla white—petals three, spreading, ovate, obtuse, nerved—stamens six, filaments short, anthers oblong, styles three, stigmas recurved.

This is the most desirable species of the genus and a very handsome herbaceous plant, the beautiful white flowers forming a pleasing contrast to the dark green leaves by which they are surrounded. It is a native of Upper Canada, and according to Nuttall, is found generally in umbrageous forests. —a peat soil, and shady situation are essential to its favorable cultivation, and as these are afforded, the flower varies accordingly in size—it is a plant of slow growth, not hearing frequent removal, and is therefore not common, though it has been known in this country since the year 1799—flowers about April, and is increased by parting the roots. The other species are not particularly desirable, except in extensive herbaceous collections.

T. sessile.	erectum.
— cernuum.	stylosum.

Plate 25. *Salpiglossis picta.*

Drawn from Nature by M.R.

Engraved by R. Havell Junr.

S A L P I G L O S S I S Picta.

Painted Salpiglossis.

Class and Order.—Didynamia Angiospermia.

Syn. Salpiglossis Picta. *Sweets B. F. G. vol.* 3. *p.* 258.

Root fibrous, stem erect, branching, lower leaves broadly lanceolate, margins deeply serrate—cauline leaves sessile, linear, acute, margins slightly undulate, becoming smaller as they approach the flower—peduncles long, leafy, flowers terminal—calyx five segments, acute—corolla beautifully pencilled with yellow and purple, funnel shaped, tube long, limb spreading, five segments, emarginate—stamens four, two long and two short—anthers large, yellow—style longer than the stamens—stigma obtuse, whole plant villous.

The genus Salpiglossis is one of late introduction into this country, none of the species being known here before the year 1826, when seeds were sent from Chili by Mr. Cruikshanks to the Botanic Gardens of Edinburgh and Glasgow. The species figured is perhaps the most beautiful, and promises to be a great acquisition to our collection of new herbaceous plants, it may be raised from seeds or cuttings, likes a light soil, and a sheltered situation, and will continue in flower for a considerable time. It has hitherto been treated chiefly as a green-house plant, but it will grow much stronger, and the colours finer, in the open border; it would, however, be desirable to keep some plants in a green-house or frame during the winter, as it is doubtful how it may bear the severe frosts. There are only two other species,

S. straminea.

— atro-purpurea.

Plate 26. *Iris variegata.*

Drawn from Nature by M.R.   *Engraved by R. Havell Junr.*

IRIS VARIEGATA.

Variegated Iris.

Class and Order.—TRIANDRIA MONOGYNIA.

Syn. Iris Variegata. *Curt. Bot. Mag. pl.* 16.

Root tuberose, cespitose,—leaves radical, clasping the stem, ensiform, nerved, unequal,—stem branched,—flower growing between two membranous green bractes, ovate, lanceolate,—tube greenish,—corolla six petals, three outer segments reflexed, oblong, obtuse, beautifully striated, and fringed at the base with glandular hairs,—three inner ones yellow, erect, margins undulate,—stamens three, filaments adhering to the base of the reflexed petals, apex bifid,—anthers oblong,—style slender,—stigma divided into three parts.

This species of Iris, though so long since introduced as the year 1597 is not frequently seen in our herbaceous collections. It is a plant of low growth, sometimes not exceeding a foot in height, though this varies according to the soil in which it is planted, a moist situation increasing its luxuriance both in flower and foliage. It is a native of Hungary, and is perfectly hardy, not requiring any particular treatment, and may be increased by separating the roots in Autumn,—flowers in May, and grows best in a stiff cold soil. This is a very beautiful genus, and affords many ornamental species.

I. pallida.	dichotoma.
— nipalensis.	pumila.
— ochroleuca.	xiphium.
— flavecens.	xiphioides.
— verna.	versicolor.
— cristata.	caucasica.
— germanica.	furcata.
— aphylla.	tenax.

Plate 27. *Delphinium grandiflorum.*

Drawn from Nature by M.R.

Engraved by R. Havell Junr.

DELPHINIUM Grandiflorum.

Great flowered Larkspur.

Class and Order.—Polyandria Trigynia.

Syn. Delphinium Grandiflorum. *Curt. Bot. Mag. pl.* 1686.

Root fibrous,—stem erect, much branched,—radical leaves on long naked petioles, multipartite, segments narrow acute,—cauline leaves sessile, verticillate, linear acute, on the lateral branches, generally single,—lower flowers on very long peduncles—calyx none—corolla very brilliant blue—outer petals five, ovate, undulate, upper one terminated by a long rugose spur—nectaries two, divided into four segments, the two lower ones marked with a bright bearded yellow spot, enclosing the parts of fructification—stamens numerous—styles three—capsules three celled.

The genus Delphinium is a beautiful and showy one, and contains almost innumerable varieties, none, however, can exceed in beauty of colour the species figured, which is a native of Siberia, and was introduced into this country about the year 1741. It is a hardy plant, of the easiest culture, not requiring any particular treatment, though it grows best in a rich brown loam—if allowed to sow its seed, a number of young plants will soon appear, which will flower the next year; this mode, however, of propagating it, is by no means certain, and therefore, in order to obtain it true, it is better to divide the roots, which may be done in spring; numerous and very beautiful varieties are constantly raised from seed. Amongst the most desirable distinct species are

D. Aconiti. pallidum.
— cheilanthum. pictum.
— macranthon. Menziesii.

— alpinum.   montanum.
— azureum.   ucranicum.

Pl. 27.

Plate 28. *Lilium concolor.*

Drawn from Nature by M.R. **Engraved by R. Havell Jun[r.]**

LILIUM Concolor.

Self-coloured Chinese Lily.

Class and Order.—HEXANDRIA MONOGYNIA.

Syn. Lilium Concolor.   *Par. Lond. tab.* 47.
— Lilium Concolor.   *Curt. Bot. Mag. pl.* 1165.

Root bulbous, squamose—stem erect, leafy, two feet high or more—leaves alternate, nerved, sessile, linear lanceolate—peduncles axillary, one flowered—corolla bright scarlet, tube short—petals six, lanceolate, recurved when the flower is fully expanded—stamens six, shorter than the petals—filaments erect, anthers oblong, germen green, style thick, as if composed of three parts, stigma trifid.

This is one of the most beautiful species of the genus Lilium. It is rare, perhaps from the difficulty that attends its cultivation, the bulbs being extremely liable to be lost in the winter from severe frosts or damp; it is a native of China, and was introduced into this country in the year 1806. A sheltered situation, and light rich soil, mixed with bog, are necessary for it, and it is increased by off-sets, which are produced in tolerable abundance. All the species of Lilium are desirable for a flower garden.

L. japonicum.   pyrenaicum.
— candidum.   pomponium.
— bulbiferum.   carolinianum.
— aurantiacum.   tigrinum.
— Catesbœi.   pumilum.
— philadelphicum.   longiflorum.
— canadense.   spectabile.
— superbum.   croceum.
— chalcedonicum.   prœcox.

Plate 29. *Penstemon ovatus.*

Drawn from Nature by M.R. **Engraved by R. Havell Junr.**

PENSTEMON Ovatus.

Ovate-leaved Penstemon.

Class and Order.—DIDYNAMIA ANGIOSPERMIA.

Syn. Penstemon ovatus. *Curt. Bot. Mag. N. S. pl.* 2903.

Root fibrous, stem erect, two or three feet high—cauline leaves sessile, amplexicaul at the base, cordate, margins dentate, becoming smaller and entire as they approach the summit—radical leaves, large, ovate, dentate, on long channelled petioles—flowers in fascicles, which are axillary—calyx five segments, equal, lanceolate acute—corolla bilabiate, tube purple, lip bright blue, upper lip erect, divided into two segments, three lower reflexed—throat hairy—stamens four, two long, and two short, curved—one barren filament, with an acute claw at the base, apex hairy, style recurved—leaves, when young, of a beautiful purple on the under side.

Great additions have lately been made to this genus, by Mr. Douglas, who has discovered many new and valuable plants in North America, among which is the species figured. According to the Bot. Mag. pl. 2903, N. S. it was found by him "growing plentifully among the limestone rocks on the high mountains about the grand rapids of the Columbia river, at the distance of 140 miles from the ocean," and sent to the Hort. Soc. in 1826; it likes a light loam and sheltered situation, and may be increased by seeds or parting the roots. When well grown it is a very beautiful and elegant plant, and a great acquisition to the flower garden. As we are yet scarcely aware how it may bear the cold of our winters, it will be desirable to protect it from severe frosts. The genus can now boast of many new and beautiful species,

P. speciosum.	Richardsonii.
— glandulosum.	procerum.
— prunosum.	glaucum.
— roseum.	venustum.
— pulchellum.	angustifolium.
— campanulatum.	digitalis.
— confertum.	

Plate 30. Geum Quellyon.
Drawn from Nature by M.R.
Engraved by R. Havell Jun.

GEUM Quellyon.

Chili Avens.

Class and Order.—ICOSANDRIA POLYGNIA.

Syn. Geum Quellyon.	*Sweet's B. F. G. p.* 292.
— Geum Coccinium.	*Bot. Reg.* 1088.

Root fibrous—radical leaves growing in a tuft, large, lobed, lyrate, interruptedly pinnate, terminal leaflet cordate, margin dentate; side leaflets numerous, sessile, becoming smaller to the base—cauline leaves sessile, pinnatifed—flowers stem radical, erect, branching—stipules ovate, acute—peduncles leafy—flowers terminal—calyx five segments, reflexed, acute—petals five, bright scarlet, nearly round, emarginate, obtuse—stamens numerous—radiated filaments inserted in the tube of the calyx, anthers yellow, styles many, germen superior—whole plant hairy.

This beautiful plant is a very valuable acquisition to our flower borders, from the brilliancy of its colour, and affording a continued succession of flowers. Mr. Sweet, and some of the Continental Botanists consider the specific name "Coccineum," which has been applied to it, as confusing it with the plant known by that name in the "Flora Græca," which, it is supposed, has never been introduced into this country, it appears of much lower growth than the one now figured, with orange flowers, and the terminal leaflet a great deal larger. The species before us is a native of Chili, where it is called "Quellyon" by the inhabitants, who use the root for medicinal purposes. It is a plant of easy cultivation, growing in any common garden soil, and is readily increased by seeds or parting the roots; introduced into this country about the year 1826. There are only two other species worth attention for the flower garden.

G. montanum.
— atlanticum.

Plate 31. Verbena chamœdryfolia.

Drawn from Nature by M.R.

Engraved by R. Havell Jun.ʳ

VERBENA Chamædryfolia.

Scarlet flowered Vervain.

Class and Order.—Didynamia Angiospernia.

Syn. Verbena chamædryfolia.	*Persoon's Syn. vol. 2. p.* 138.
— Verbena chamædryfolia.	*Sweet's B. F. G. 2d series, p.* 9.
— Verbena melindres.	*Bot. Reg. pl.* 1184.

Root fibrous, stem prostrate, branching—leaves opposite, sessile, oblong, ovate, margins deeply serrate, hairy on both sides—flowers terminal, corymbose—calyx campanulate, five cleft—corolla very bright crimson, tubular, limb spreading, five segments, obtuse emarginate—throat white, hairy—stamens four, two long, two short, inserted in the tube of the corolla—anthers two lobed, style one, smooth, stigma bifid, germen smooth.

The unrivalled brilliancy of the colour of this beautiful species of Verbena, renders it a most ornamental plant for the front of the flower borders, and when grown in large patches it is almost impossible to give an idea of the dazzling splendour of its appearance; it is a plant of the easiest cultivation, and if allowed to grow according to its natural habit, which is prostrate, it will propagate itself by the radicles which are produced at the different joints, and by this means will attach itself to the ground; the plants thus rooted may be removed any time. A brown loamy soil, a good deal of moisture, and a sheltered situation are necessary, and as it is doubtful how it may bear the severity of our winters, it is the safest method to keep some plants in a frame, during severe frosts, which will flower early in the ensuing spring. It is a native of Paraguay and Buenos Ayres, and was introduced into this country about 1827. There are only two other species worth cultivating in the flower garden.

> V. aubletia.
> — pulchella.

Plate 32. *Linum Narbonense.*

Drawn from Nature by M.R.   *Engraved by R. Havell Jun[r.]*

L I N U M Narbonense.

Narbonne Flax.

Class and Order.—Pentandria Pentagynia.

Syn. Linum Narbonense. *Persoon's Syn. vol.* 1. *p.* 334.

Root fibrous,—stem branching,—leaves sessile, alternate, linear acute, smooth, glaucous,—flowers terminal on moderate peduncles,—calyx five segments, linear acute,—corolla bright blue, beautifully vein'd, with a darker shade,—petals five, obovate, margins slightly undulate,—stamens five, anthers oblong, filaments united at the base, surrounding the germen, which is crowned by five thread-like styles.

This is perhaps the finest and most beautiful species of Linum, and bears the largest flowers of any of the hardy kinds. It is a very desirable garden plant, continuing long in bloom, and forming a pleasing variety from its glaucous foilage. It is a native of Spain, Italy, and the south of France, and was introduced into this country about the year 1759; though we are not aware that any figure of it has before been given. This species may be raised from seed, which is produced in abundance; if sown in light rich soil, and protected through the winter, the young plants will flower the following summer, and attain the height of eighteen inches or two feet when in perfection. It is very hardy—this genus does not afford many ornamental species for a flower garden, the most desirable are,

    L. perenne.
    — alpina.
    — flavum.

Plate 41. *Tigridia conchiflora.*

Drawn from Nature by M.R.

Engraved by R. Havell Junr.

TIGRIDIA Conchiflora.

Yellow-flowered Tigridia.

Class and Order.—TRIANDRIA MONOGYNIA.

Syn. Tigridia Conchiflora. *Sweet's B. F. G. t.* 128.

Root bulbous—stem radical, angular—leaves alternate, broadly lanceolate, plicate, inflated at the base, dark green, two sheathing spathes at the base of the corolla, ovate, lanceolate—corolla bright orange, slightly tinted with a redder shade on the margin of the petals, base spotted with dark crimson—petals six, three outer petals broadly ovate, acute, base concave, three inner ones smaller, panduriform—stamens three—filaments united—anthers oblong—style longer than the stamens—stigma divided into three parts, each bifid.

This is one of the most splendid plants which has been introduced into this country. It is a native of Mexico, and was brought thence by Mr. Bullock, in 1824. On its first flowering here, it was considered a variety only of T. pavonia, but upon careful examination they appeared to be perfectly distinct. This is satisfactorily proved by Mr. Sweet, in his B. F. G. p. 128. The bulbs may be planted early in the spring in light sandy soil, and placed in a green-house or frame, as it facilitates their flowering: when the weather permits, the roots should be taken out of the pots and put into the open air, in a warm sheltered situation, where they will make a brilliant appearance for a considerable time—when they have done flowering, the roots require to be taken up and kept dry during the winter. The only species with which we are yet acquainted, besides the one figured, is T. pavonia.

Pl. 41.

Plate 42. Colchicum Byzantinum.
Drawn from Nature by M.R.

Jun^(r.)   *Engraved by R. Havell*

COLCHICUM Byzantinum.

Broad-leaved Meadow Saffron.

Class and Order.—Hexandria Trigynia.

Syn. Colchicum byzantinum.	*Bot. Mag. pl.* 1122.
— Colchicum byzantinum.	*Sweet's Hort. Brit. p.* 539.

Root bulbous, very large—scape radical, many flowered—corolla lilac pink—tube long, petals six, ob-ovate, spreading, strongly nerved at the back of each petal, tipped with a deeper color—stamens six, three longer than the others—filaments inserted in the base of the petals—anthers bright yellow—styles three, longer than the stamens—leaves radical, very large, broadly lanceolate, plicate, smooth, appearing after the flowers decay.

There cannot be a greater ornament to the flower garden in the autumnal months than the C. byzantinum, which is the finest species of the genus. We learn from the Bot. Mag. that, in 1598, bulbs of this plant were received by Clusius, at Vienna, from Constantinople, but it was not until 1629 that it was introduced into this country. It is a native of the Levant, and is perfectly hardy, not requiring any particular mode of treatment, except being planted in a light soil, mixed with bog. The flowers appear about September, but the leaves, which are the largest of any of the species, do not arrive at maturity until the following spring. The C. autumnale is famed for its medicinal properties. This is not a numerous genus; the most desirable species are

         C. crociflorum.
         — autumnale.
         — var. white.
         — variegatum.

Pl. 42.

Plate 43. *Helianthus atrorubens.*

Drawn from Nature by M.R. Junr.

Engraved by R. Havell

HELIANTHUS Atrorubens.

Dark-eyed Sunflower.

Class and Order.—Syngenesia Polygamia Frustrania.

Syn. Helianthus atrorubens.   *Pursh Flo. N. A. vol.* 2, *p.* 573.
— Helianthus atrorubens.   *Bot. Mag. pl.* 2668.

Root fibrous—stem tall, erect, branching—radical leaves very large, broadly lanceolate, margins dentate, nerved, of a dark green—cauline leaves sessile, opposite, ovate lanceolate, dentate acute—calyx many segments imbricate, acute—corolla dark bright yellow—radiated florets, barren dentate—florets of the disk fertile—whole plant rugose.

This is perhaps one of the most desirable species of the genus Helianthus, from the brilliancy of the colour and its moderate growth. It makes a striking appearance when planted at the back of the flower borders, and will continue in beauty to a late period in the autumn. According to Pursh it is found in the "western parts of Pennsylvania," and was introduced into this country in 1732. It will grow well in any good garden soil, and may be increased by parting the roots. There are not many species of this genus suitable for a flower garden, as they grow to such a large size, and take up so much room: the best are

        H. mollis.
        — multiflorus.
        — diffusus.

Plate 44. *Lupinus mutabilis.*
Drawn from Nature by M.R.
Engraved by R. Havell Junr.

LUPINUS Mutabilis.

Changeable-flowered Lupin.

Class and Order.—DIADELPHIA DECANDRIA.

Syn. Lupinus mutabilis.	*Bot. Mag. pl.* 2682.
— Lupinus mutabilis.	*Sweet's B. F. G. vol.* 2, *p.* 130.

Root fibrous—stem suffruticose, branching, smooth—leaves on long petioles, digitate; leaflets (generally nine) oblong, mucronate—spike lateral—flowers verticillate, on short pedicels, white, changing to a beautiful purple as decay approaches—calyx two segments; upper segment erect, emarginate; lower one acute—vexillum nearly round, sides reflexed, yellow at the base—alæ broad obtuse—carina acute, enclosing the parts of fructification—stamens ten—filaments united at the base, concealing the germen—style a little longer than the stamens—stigma very small—legumen broad, margin deeply undulate, containing generally three white smooth seeds.

The genus Lupinus is now become very interesting, from the numerous fine species that have lately been introduced; none can exceed in beauty the one here figured, which possesses a peculiar attraction from its flowers being most beautiful when in a state of decay. According to the Bot. Mag. p. 2682, it was "raised from seeds received by Mr. Barclay, from Bogota, in Columbia, and communicated in flower in August 1826." There is no doubt it will soon be generally cultivated, as it bears seeds in abundance, which may be sown in good rich soil in the open ground, and the plants thus reared will flower abundantly during the summer months, and continue in beauty till destroyed by frost. It is yet uncertain whether this species be more than annual. Amongst the finest of this genus are

L. polyphyllus.	L. nootkatensis.
— canaliculatus.	— perennis.
— versicolor.	— lepidus.
— bicolor.	
— leucophyllus.	

Plate 45. *Papaver nudicaule.*

Drawn from Nature by M.R.   **Engraved by R. Havell Jun.ʳ**

PAPAVER Nudicaule.

Naked-stalked Poppy.

Class and Order.—Polyandria Monogynia.

Syn. Papaver nudicaule.	*Hort. Kew. vol. 3. p.* 289.
— Papaver nudicaule.	*Bot. Mag. pl.* 1633.

Root fibrous—leaves radical, clustered, on long channelled petioles, pinnatifid, hairy—stem radical, naked, erect when the flower expands, hairy—flower terminal—calyx two segments, concave, deciduous—corolla very pale yellow—petals four spreading, orbicular, margins crenate—stamens numerous, inserted into the receptacle—anthers dark yellow—style cylindrical—stigma stellate.

Though this species of Papaver cannot boast of brilliancy of colour, it is nevertheless a very lovely plant from its delicacy and simplicity; and, from the continued succession of flowers, it will be found an ornamental plant to our gardens. According to the Hort. Kew. p. 289, "it is a native of Norway and Siberia, and was cultivated in 1730 by Dr. James Sherard." Numerous beautiful varieties have been raised from seed, which make a very gay appearance all through the summer and autumn, until checked by frost: these are quite hardy, and will grow in any light rich soil. The most ornamental species are

P. bracteatum.	rubro-aurantiacum.
— alpinum.	orientale.
— crocea.	

Pl. 45.

Plate 46. *Gladiolus Cardinalis.*

Drawn from Nature by M.R.

Junr·

Engraved by R. Havell

GLADIOLUS Cardinalis.

Superb Corn-flag.

Class and Order.—Triandria Monogynia.

Syn. Gladiolus Cardinalis. *Bot. Mag. t.* 135.

Root bulbous—leaves radical, embracing the stem at the base, linear, lanceolate, striate—scape sometimes two feet in height, drooping, many-flowered—calyx two sheath-like segments, lanceolate, acute—corolla bright scarlet, monopetalous, campanulate, tube long, limb six segments, irregular, oblong, ovate, margins undulate; three smaller segments beautifully marked with a white stripe on the centre of each—stamens three—filaments long, inserted in the tube of the corolla—anthers oblong—style longer than the stamens—stigma divided into three parts.

It is almost impossible to give an adequate representation of the brilliant colour of this beautiful species of Gladiolus, which was introduced into this country from Holland, about the year 1789, by the gardener to the King of Naples: though generally considered a tender plant, it will be found to grow well out of doors, in a southern aspect and sheltered situation, only requiring protection in the winter to keep the roots from severe frosts. Many of the bulbs from the Cape of Good Hope, of which place this is a native, may be grown well with care and attention in the open air, and make a beautiful addition to the flower garden in the summer months. The bulbs should be planted six or eight inches deep in a rich sandy soil, in a south aspect, where they will grow strong and flower freely. The hardiest species are

G. tristis.

— byzantinus.

— communis.
— carneus.
— segetum.

Pl. 46.

Plate 47. Commelina cœlestis.

Drawn from Nature by M.R.   **Engraved by R. Havell Junr.**

COMMELINA Cœlestis.

Sky-blue Commelina.

Class and Order.—TRIANDRIA MONOGYNIA.

Syn. Commelina Cœlestis.   *Sweet's B. F. G. t. 3.*
— Commelina Cœlestis.   *Rœmer et Schultz, sys. veg. v. 1. p. 533.*
— Commelina Cœlestis.   *Wild Enumer, vol. 1. p. 61.*

Root tuberous, fasciculated, fusiform—stem erect, branching—leaves smooth, ovate, lanceolate, striate, margins undulate, base concave, sheathing the stem, fringed on one side with a line of hairs—peduncle pubescent—flower terminal—involucrum cordate, acute, enclosing two or more flowers—pedicel smooth, very short—calyx three segments, alternate with the petals—corolla bright blue—petals three, equal, ovate, margins undulate—nectaries three, erect—stamens three—filaments recurved—anthers sagittate—style longer than the stamens—stigma very small.

Though this plant is frequently confused with C. tuberosa it is proved to be decidedly distinct, Mr. Sweet having obligingly informed the author that he has carefully compared the two species, and thus confirmed the opinions of Rœmer et Schultz, and other botanists on the Continent, where the distinction is now generally adopted. This species, which has a larger and lighter coloured flower, longer and narrower leaves, than C. tuberosa, is a native of Mexico, and was introduced into this country in 1813: it has been generally treated as a green-house plant, but it will grow perfectly well in the open air, though from the fleshy nature of the roots it is necessary to take them up in winter, and treat them in the same manner as Dahlias. C. crassifolia is the only species besides the two above mentioned, suitable for the flower garden.

Pl. 47.

Plate 48. *Sternbergia lutea.*
Drawn from Nature by M.R.

Engraved by R. Havell Junr.

STERNBERGIA Lutea.

Yellow Sternbergia.

Class and Order.—Hexandria Monogynia.

Syn. Sternbergia Lutea.	*Sweet's Hort. Brit. p.* 505.
— Amaryllis Lutea.	*Bot. Mag. t.* 290.

Root bulbous—leaves radical, broadly linear, channelled, obtuse, dark green, lighter underneath—scape one-flowered, seven or eight inches high—spathe ovate, lanceolate—corolla yellow—six petals, oblong, obtuse, margin entire—stamens six—filaments inserted at the base of the petals—anthers oblong—style one—stigma very small—germen large.

This plant, formerly known as Amaryllis lutea, is a native of the South of Europe, and various parts of the East. Though introduced into this country as early as 1596, it is by no means common. When planted in the front of the borders it is very ornamental, particularly when exposed to a bright sun, which causes the flowers to expand. It has acquired a more interesting character, from the supposition entertained by the late Sir J. E. Smith, that it may possibly be the Lily of Scripture, to which we find such beautiful allusions in the Sacred writings. Sir J. E. S. observes, "It is natural to presume the Divine Teacher, according to his usual custom, called the attention of his hearers to some object at hand; and, as the fields of the Levant are overrun with the Amaryllis lutea, whose golden liliaceous flowers in Autumn afford one of the most brilliant and gorgeous objects in nature, the expression of 'Solomon, in all his glory, not being arrayed like one of these,' is peculiarly appropriate." It is a plant of easy cultivation, perfectly hardy, and will grow in any good garden soil. At present there are few species of this genus.

S. colchiciflora.
— Clusiana.

www.ingramcontent.com/pod-product-compliance
Lightning Source LLC
Chambersburg PA
CBHW081115080526
44587CB00021B/3609